Short Stories on Character

The Bible Tells Me So Press

Short Stories on Character
Book 2

A children's book produced by
The Bible Tells Me So Press

PUBLISHED BY
THE BIBLE TELLS ME SO CORPORATION
WWW.THEBIBLETELLSMESO.COM

First Edition, September 2022

TABLE OF CONTENTS

Practice, Practice, Practice

DILIGENT

To be diligent is to work in a responsible and consistent way.
A diligent person works seriously and
focuses on the work until it is done.

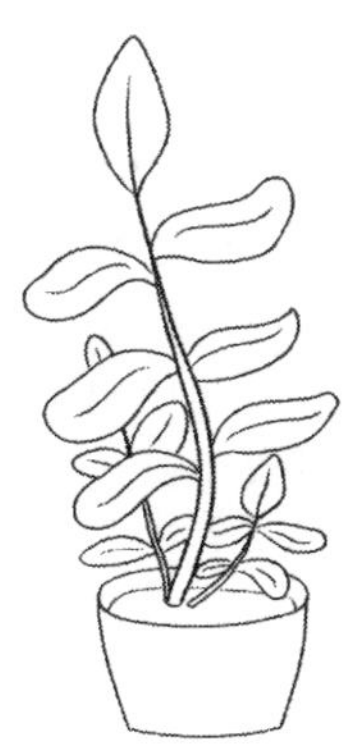

Running into the house, Jessica landed heavily on the couch, hoping to get a few minutes of rest before heading back outside to ride her new bike around the block again. She loved riding her bike, especially on days as beautiful as today.

"Before you go back outside, I want you to practice your scales on the piano," Mom called from the next room.

"Oh, Mom! It's so nice outside. Do I really have to practice piano today?" groaned Jessica.

Mom came and stood next to Jessica on the couch, "After your piano lesson yesterday, Mrs. Cummings told us you should practice thirty minutes every day, remember?"

"Thirty minutes? Every day? I'm doomed! I'll never get to ride my new bike again!" sighed Jessica, closing her eyes and lowering her head in despair.

Mom smiled, "Now, now, Jessica, it's not as bad as you make it sound. Thirty minutes will go by faster than you think."

"Okay, Mom," Jessica replied dutifully, "but I still think I'm doomed and that this whole beautiful day is doomed as well." To which Mom knowingly and lovingly replied, "We'll see, my dear. We'll see..."

Jessica dragged her feet as she slowly walked over to the piano and slumped down on the stool. Then, she reluctantly turned the pages of her exercise book to the scales she needed to practice.

"Better get started, Jessica," called Mom from the kitchen. "Here,

I'll set the kitchen timer for 30 minutes. When it goes off, you'll be all done for the day."

"Well, I guess I should try to make the most of it," thought Jessica, as she looked at the finger placement chart and carefully put her fingers on the right keys. She straightened her posture and began playing up the scale: C-D-E-F-G-A-B-C. Then she went back down the scale again, mumbling the names of the keys softly to herself as she played them.

Again and again she rippled her fingers across the keys, each time playing the notes a little smoother than the time before. Then, the tones began to warm and cascade gently through the house, filling every room with a smile.

Even Jessica felt a bit surprised that she was actually beginning to enjoy practicing the piano. Sure, she was only playing some simple little scales, but she found that the more effort she put into making each note sound as nice as possible, the more these simple little scales began to sound really nice. Then, she practiced and practiced until she was playing the scales without even looking at her hands. She was even turning the scales into songs by singing the names of each note as she played them. As she practiced all these delightful little scales, she lost track of the time.

"Beep! Beep! Beep!" When the buzzer sounded, Jessica scampered into the kitchen to turn it off. Mom looked up from scrubbing potatoes. "Impressive! How did that go for you?" she asked.

"Not too bad!" beamed Jessica, grabbing an apple.

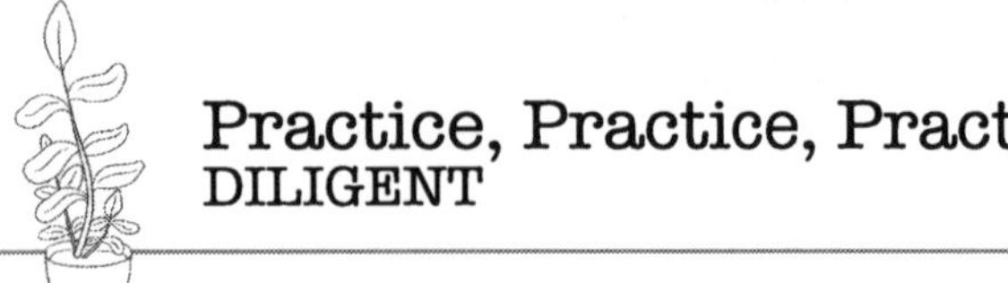

"It's not easy to build up a new habit," said Mom with an encouraging smile. "It takes diligence, and you keep at it every day, even when you don't feel like it. Keep it up, Jessica! Now you still have plenty of time to ride your bike and enjoy the rest of this beautiful day."

"Thanks, Mom!" Jessica called, as she spilled out the front door. The apple crunched in her mouth, and the notes still flowed through her head.

It really was a beautiful day.

Bible Verse

Go to the ant,
you sluggard;
consider
its ways,
and be wise.

Proverbs 6:6

Family Talk Time!

In this story Jessica diligently practiced her piano until she was done. Although she would have preferred to ride her bike outside, her mom helped her realize she needed to be consistent with her practicing. There are a lot of things we do each day that require diligence. Every day you have to make your bed and clean up your room. Every day you need to get your homework done. When you do these things in a consistent, responsible way, it will help you to become diligent. Diligent people do what they are supposed to do when they are supposed to do it!

Things to consider...

1. What is diligence?

2. How did Jessica react when her mom asked her to practice the piano?

3. What things do you do diligently every day?

4. In what areas do you need more diligence?

A Big-Hearted Baseball Game

BROAD

To be broad is to have a heart that includes others.
A broad person doesn't form exclusive groups
but cares for everyone in the same way.

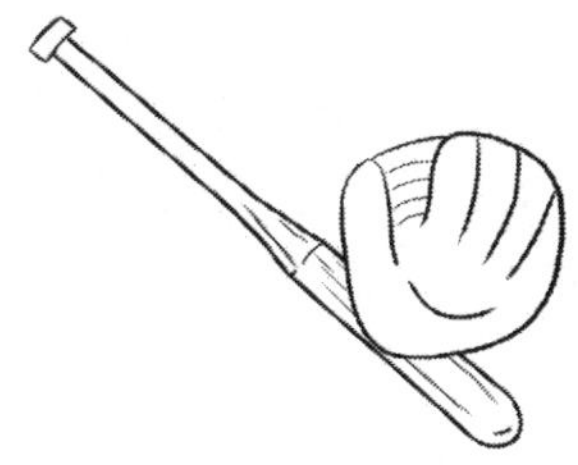

Smack! Ezra whacked the baseball with a mighty swing. He slid hard into second base, almost missing the base completely. At that very moment John caught the relay throw and lunged forward with the tag to Ezra's shoulder. But it was too late!

"I'm safe!" squealed Ezra as he slipped his hand under John's outstretched glove. And he was. It was such a thrill to play baseball with all the boys in his fourth grade P.E. class. When the game was over, they trudged back to class together, slapping each other on the back, wiping the sweat off their faces, and replaying all the best moments. After school the boys laughed and joked on their way home about how everyone had played.

"We'll play another game in P.E. tomorrow!" Ezra called, waving good-bye as he turned his bike down his street. Just as he broke off from the pack, John called out after him, "Wait, Ezra, let's play again today at 5! And bring your big swing, too!" "Okay!" Ezra yelled back excitedly. "Let me just check in at home, but I should be able to play after I get my homework done!"

With a broad smile he pedaled hard toward home. Then he saw his younger sister Sarah and her friends gathered outside with their bats, gloves, and wiffle balls. He tried to pass unnoticed. But it was too late—they spotted him and called out, "Hey, Ezra! When you finish your homework, can you play baseball with us? Please?" "Oh no!" thought Ezra. "Now what am I going to do?"

"Ummmm...I've got a lot of homework," Ezra replied. "Let me see if my mom will let me." And he ducked out of sight into the garage. Of course he remembered his friends, and he didn't really want to play baseball with all these younger kids. Ezra found his mother in the kitchen chopping vegetables.

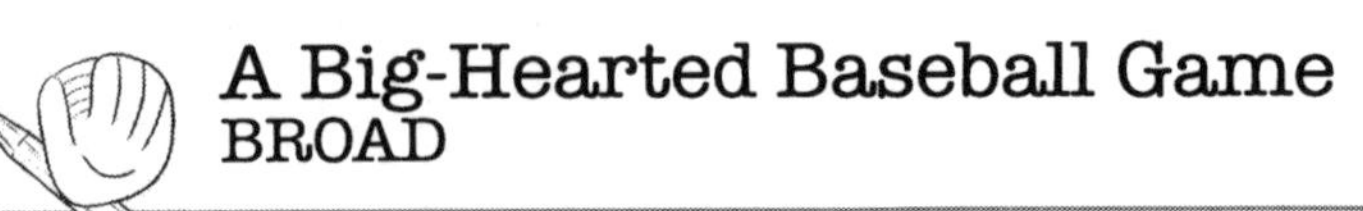

"Here, son, have a carrot," she said cheerfully in his direction. "How was school today?"

"It was great!" Ezra replied, munching thoughtfully. "I hit a double. My friends want to play more before dinner; it's just..." Mom set a drink beside him and sat down to listen. "Yes?" she asked softly as Ezra shifted uncomfortably. "Well, Sarah and her friends...they saw me, and they want me to play with them."

"I see," Mom answered, nodding slowly. "And you were maybe hoping for more baseball with your pals?" Ezra nodded, and Mom continued. "And you really don't want to play with the younger kids?" Ezra looked down bashfully. "Well, not really, Mom; they always mess up and stuff." Mom sat back in her chair and was quiet a moment while Ezra started his second carrot.

"Ezra," she said finally, "son, you are growing so big. I'm really impressed. And I'm sure your sister is too. She and her friends just look up to your positive example. It would be something really special to include them. This is to have a broad heart, and it's really important."

By this point Ezra stopped chewing and looked up at his mom. It was clear that her words were getting through to him. She looked out the back patio and added, "A broad heart doesn't exclude others but cares for everyone and considers everyone. Besides, just think how happy this will make them. And you'll be the happiest!"

"Thanks, Mom," Ezra smiled as he rushed through the door to ask the younger kids to join his game with his friends. He couldn't believe how excited everyone was as they squealed and giggled into

the house. He headed to his room with his homework, and promptly at 5 o'clock, they all crowded down to the school yard.

John and Mark were already there, and their eyes were wide with disbelief. Ezra let them know the plan, and John pulled him to the side. "Hey, why are they here? They're little kids." By now Mark had joined the huddle with a scowl on his face.

"Look, guys," Ezra answered positively. "They really want to play, and we should just include them. It's the right thing to do." John and Mark shrugged and reluctantly agreed, and then Ezra let the girls choose which positions they wanted. "Thanks for not sticking us all in right field," laughed Stephanie, as she headed over to third base.

Tossing the baseball into his glove, Ezra took the mound and surveyed the whole field with his team behind him. All the smiling faces looked back, and just for a moment his heart seemed to swell from within. Mom was right; he was the happiest player on the field.

Bible Verse

And God gave Solomon... largeness of heart, even as the sand that is on the seashore.

1 Kings 4:29

Family Talk Time!

In this story we see how Ezra was broad, or big-hearted. Although he could have played baseball only with his friends, he chose to include his younger sister's friends too. When you are at school or on the playground, and someone whom you may not prefer to play with would like to join in, you should make an effort to welcome them. By doing this, you will become a broad person.

Things to consider...

1. In what ways was Ezra big-hearted or broad?

2. What was his initial reaction when Sarah's friends asked him to play with them?

3. How do you think Ezra felt after including the younger kids?

4. What are some other ways we can show that we have a broad heart?

Every Last Block

FINE

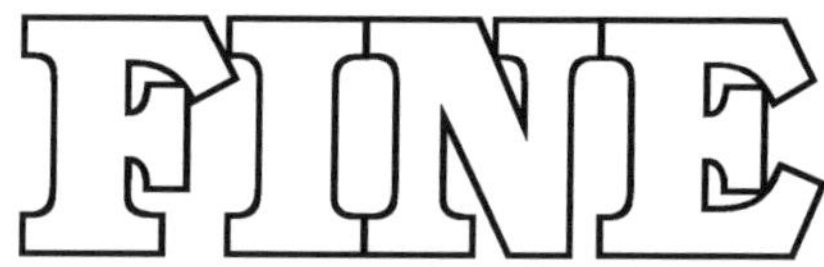

To be fine means to be careful and detailed, not careless or negligent. If we are fine persons, we will be able to complete assignments given to us, and others can entrust us with bigger, more important tasks.

Sprawled out on the living room rug with his bucket of building blocks, Jacob was busy building a castle. Playing with blocks was one of his favorite rainy day activities. He carefully selected the flat blocks first to make the base, and then he gathered the square ones for the tower. "I wonder how high I could make it?" he thought to himself.

Just as Jacob finished the tower, Dad called through the back patio door. "Jacob, do you want to go with me to the hardware store?"

"All right!" replied Jacob. "Yes, I do! But Dad...look at what I've been working on."

Dad stepped in and surveyed the castle with approval. "Wow, you did all that? I loved to build castles with your uncle when we were your age. We used to build towers up to the ceiling!"

"Really? I want to try to make my castle that high when we get back from the hardware store. But...how can we keep Sarah from knocking down what I've already done while we are away?"

Scanning the living room quickly, Dad said, "No problem. I'll ask Mom to keep an eye on Sarah. But before we go, you have to pick up all these extra blocks." Jacob nodded, and Dad disappeared upstairs.

Jacob thought to himself, "Hmm. I wonder if I can just pick up the ones I can see. That will be good enough. I don't think Dad will notice."

Five minutes later Dad was back with his keys in his hand. "Are

you ready to go, son?" he asked cheerfully.

Jacob tossed a couple more blocks into the bucket and kicked two more over next to it. "Almost," he said, shrugging.

Dad paused, and his keys became quiet. He leaned down low to check under the couch and the coffee table. "Almost, huh?" he replied. "Jacob, I see a lot more blocks under here."

Jacob followed his father's gaze but didn't really want to take more time now. "Besides," he thought, "I'll be using them again later." Then he said out loud, "Well...I was just thinking, you know, to get those when we come back."

Dad was on his knees now and pulled Jacob in close from behind. His head rested on Jacob's shoulder, and they both looked at the scattered blocks. "Hmm, you were thinking all that?" he said right into Jacob's ear with a small laugh in his voice. "I just wonder what Mom would be thinking about that?"

Jacob began to laugh because of Dad's funny voice, and they both knew what Mom had asked them about the living room many times. "I think she would say," Jacob answered, grinning but also sheepishly, "we're supposed to always put everything away before we start something else."

"Or?" Dad replied, releasing Jacob to scoot across the room toward the couch.

"Or if we leave the house," Jacob answered.

Dad nodded approvingly and watched his son with pleasure. He

paused a moment more, watching the dashing about, and then between the clatter of blocks spoke softly, "That's it, Jacob. It may seem like nothing to leave some stuff for later. I sometimes want to be that way too, but I also have learned that whatever I do, do it with all of my heart to the Lord. Then, in all the little things you can be awesome."

"Okay, Daddy," replied Jacob. "But can you help me this time?"

"Sure thing," Dad said with a smile. "I'll move the couches, and we'll get every last block into the bucket in no time!"

With everything put in order again, Jacob's dad bundled him up in his arms so they could survey the work. "Now we're ready to go," announced Dad as they backed toward the front door. And they were, thought Jacob, holding his dad close with a most satisfied smile.

Bible Verse

And how precious are Your thoughts to me, O God! How great is the sum of them!

Psalm 139:17

Family Talk Time!

In this story Jacob learns about being fine and detailed. His dad asking him to pick up ALL the blocks was teaching Jacob not to be careless even in the small things. At first, Jacob wasn't careful and detailed, but with a little reminder and help, in the end he did a thorough job, picking up even the building blocks left under the couches. We all can do things in two ways: we can either leave a job unfinished, or we can do it in a careful, detailed way. The next time you are asked to do a job, choose to complete it in a fine way.

Things to consider...

1. Was Jacob fine when he cleaned up the blocks?

2. Are you thorough when you pick up your toys or belongings?

3. Is there something you have worked on that you completed in a fine, detailed way?

4. Can Daddy or Mommy share a time they weren't thorough and what happened?

For more
books, videos, songs, and crafts,
visit us online at
TheBibleTellsMeSo.com

Standing on the Bible and growing!

Printed in Great Britain
by Amazon